The One Minute To-Do List

Michael Linenberger

New Academy Publishers
San Ramon, California

First printing 2011

ISBN-13: 978-0-9833647-0-2
ISBN-10: 0-9833647-0-2
Library of Congress Control Number: 2011913760

Visit the publisher's website at www.MichaelLinenberger.com for additional information.

The following trademarks appear throughout this book: Microsoft, Windows, Microsoft Office, Microsoft Outlook, ToodleDo, One Minute To-Do List, 1MTD, Master Your Now!, Over-the-Horizon tasks, Critical Now, Opportunity Now, Target Now, Defer-to-Do, Defer-to-Review, FRESH Prioritization.

Cover photograph of Michael Linenberger by Joe Burull

Contents

Introduction

Are You Feeling Overwhelmed?

I bet you picked up this book because you are feeling overwhelmed—either a little or a lot. Perhaps you feel that tasks and e-mail are flying in too fast and productive work is getting buried under constant emergencies. Or maybe you are even feeling that your workday is *completely* out of control—that you are behind on *everything* and hopelessly overburdened. If any of this sounds like your situation—great!

Wait, why is that *great*? Because you're going to be very happy with the amazingly rapid relief this short book will give to you. By reading only to the end of Chapter 1— just a few short pages away—you will gain significant order in your chaotic workday and enjoy a refreshing contrast with your present state. Then, by reading just a little further—through Chapter 3—you'll have mastered a set of tools that will allow you to permanently get control of your workday. The rest of the book will be icing on the cake—providing a complete system to keep you ahead of your busy workload in all situations.

By the way, don't feel bad if you *are* feeling completely overwhelmed; you're not alone. Nearly all busy people these days are overloaded with work. That's especially true given all the e-mail we get and the additional work that brings. A recent Harris poll says 80 percent of people do not like their jobs. Most people say the problem is that they are overworked—that they have too much on their plate. So, it makes sense that you feel the same way.

But there is a solution. Tens of thousands of people have gained control by using the simple to-do list approach in this book, which I call the One Minute To-Do List, and the reports are outstanding. For example, Ted Sampson says that for the first time ever he can make sense of all the work he has—he says he can see his priorities clearly and he can now master what needs to get done. Amy Brown reports that her new One Minute To-Do List has saved her *career* because she is finally able to meet the expectations of her demanding boss. James Frederick says it has even saved his *life*. How? His health was deteriorating from the stress of being constantly behind at work; he says with the One Minute To-Do List in place, that stress is now gone. These are typical results people experience from adding the simple tool taught in this book.

Why Most To-Do Lists Don't Work

Many of us attempt to use a to-do list to try to get our chaos under control. We do that hoping to gain a sense of order—and, of course, we do it to try to get things done. Gaining a sense of order is something we all hope for. We think if we can just get a clear picture of our current responsibilities, then everything will calm down and make more sense. And we hope that doing that will give us a leg up on our work.

But most people fail when creating and using a to-do list. The list usually gets too big and unbearable, or it ends up focusing on the wrong things first. When we look at a poorly created list, it just *adds* stress to our day rather than *solving* it. Because of that, most people give up on using their lists—particularly ones they create on their computer or smartphone.

But a to-do list, if properly created, *can* really help solve this problem. It's all about *prioritizing* correctly— that's what a good to-do list should do for you. But, surprisingly, almost none of them are able to help us prioritize our work correctly.

How come we fail at prioritizing?

First of all, it takes more than just making a list! You need to create a to-do list *smartly*. The knee-jerk approach—to simply list all your to-dos and put your most "important" tasks first—just doesn't work anymore, not with the high volumes of work tasks we all have these days.

And if you try to find training on this topic, good luck! You'll find that most to-do list and time management training is based on 50-year-old principles—ones that no longer work.

The core problem is that our ranking of high importance is too *broad*, so the list of high-priority items quickly gets way too big—everything looks important. Or that list seems to focus on the wrong things at the wrong times. We quickly give up with a sense that it just isn't working. And so we fall right back into a sense of frustration, overwhelm, and even guilt—guilt for not being able to keep up.

The Solution: The One Minute To-Do List

But it doesn't have to be that way. A to-do list, if done right, really *can* be the solution.

A good to-do list *can* show you what your most important next work to do is. A good to-do list approach *will* control the size of that list so you do not feel overwhelmed by it. A good to-do list system *should* help you do the work smartly and efficiently; it can make sure the work you do next is the right work. And it *can* truly get your workday under control.

In this book you will learn a simple and very effective "one minute" to-do list system that does all that. It's a to-do list that tells you clearly what you need to do next. It's a to-do list that is easy to keep up to date. It's a to-do list that won't overwhelm you. It works just right, so you'll feel in control and on top of your day.

Why do I call this a *"one minute"* to-do list? Because it takes only one minute to get started with it—to get it populated for the first time. The result is an almost immediate sense of stress relief. It also takes only one minute to review the list each time you refer to it—to see exactly what's pressing for the day and what isn't.

The benefits of this one minute system are huge. Your sense of chaos at work goes away. You'll get the right things done on time, and you won't waste time on the wrong things. The One Minute To-Do List removes uncertainty about what you need to do, and helps you focus on the right things. You end up feeling—and *being*—in control.

A Long-Proven System

By the way, this is a long-proven system—you can trust that you are using the best! The One Minute To-Do List is a simple version of the to-do list training given to tens of thousands of workers (just like you) who now have their workdays under control (just like you will!). The One Minute To-Do List is a quick implementation of a system called the Master Your Now! (MYN) system. That system is the basis of my many best-selling books, read by over

50,000 people and used in my daylong corporate seminars. But you don't need to take those. Rather, in this new book, the system you will use has been greatly simplified and succinctly presented. So, in just a few short chapters, you'll learn how to control your workday too, without long study or training.

Where the One Minute To-Do List Comes From

I developed this simple to-do list system while I was in the trenches of some very busy companies—while I was working, just like you, in a typically overloaded workplace.

I put the first version of the system in place when I was a VP at the large management consultancy firm Accenture. There, as a result of the system, I greatly increased my workday efficiency. I later enhanced the system while leading the Project Management Center of Excellence at AAA and made it standard training there. My experience as the head of all technology for the US Peace Corps helped instill my appreciation for keeping technology solutions simple, and that led to the simplicity of this system.

I first started training the system in 2006 for use specifically with Microsoft Outlook. I released a book on it that year titled *Total Workday Control Using Microsoft Outlook*. That book quickly became the #1 best-selling book on Outlook and has remained in that position to this day, five years later; the third edition of the book was released in March 2011. It teaches the full MYN system and it has changed the lives of tens of thousands of Outlook users.

I added a paper approach in 2010 in my book *Master Your Workday Now!* The month that book was released it instantly became the #1 best-selling time management book on Amazon. That book presented the paper version of this to-do list system, called the *Workday Mastery To-Do List*. You are going to learn essentially the same material, here, in just a few simple chapters.

Widely Used in Corporate America

The MYN system is now part of the standard productivity training at John Deere, Kohl's Department Stores, and at many other companies. It has been taught and is in use by many at GE, the US Coast Guard, Pfizer, Shell Oil, Microsoft, American Health Care Association, Merrill Lynch, Blue Cross Blue Shield, and in many other companies. So, as you can see, you are about to start with a proven and powerful system. And you'll get started in just a minute.

What's in This Book

My earlier books about MYN, the "parent" of this system, are 300 to 400 pages each. That's because there is a lot more material in those books than just learning how to manage a task list. But in this book, the one you are holding in your hand, I have simplified the content greatly to focus on just one thing: getting tasks under control quickly. I call this simplified version of the system the *One*

Minute To-Do List, or *1MTD* for short. I think that title really captures the quickness and power of what you are about to learn. And I present this simple system, step by step, in the chapters ahead.

Chapter by Chapter Guide

So, what's in each of the chapters ahead? And do you need to read them all?

This book was designed to be a very quick read. Within the first three chapters you'll have the core material down. In fact, you'll get instant relief just by reading Chapter 1; in that chapter I give you a 60-second quick start, showing you how to do the 1MTD quickly on paper. If your day feels chaotic right now, get going right away on that short chapter and enjoy the benefits immediately. Chapter 1 serves as the basis for the rest of the book.

In Chapter 2, I teach the *principles* behind the to-do list so you can understand why it works. Not everyone needs to read this chapter—but I hope you do; it's interesting!

In Chapter 3, I teach you some easy rules to follow that help keep this to-do list as powerful as it is. This is the last truly required chapter. If you were to make your to-do list on paper, you could stop reading here and you'd have the solution you need. But I think most people will want to learn how to automate this list on their computers, so read on!

In Chapters 4, 5, and 6, you'll learn how to automate the 1MTD. Automating it is purely optional, but doing so makes it more flexible—and more powerful. To that end, I first show you how to create the 1MTD in a simple text document. I then introduce you to software that focuses on to-do list management. I show you two of these—Microsoft Outlook's task module and a simple tool called ToodleDo—and I show you how to use each. Outlook is used in most companies and so is an obvious choice. I added the latter tool, ToodleDo, because it works on the largest variety of hardware—PCs, Macs, tablets, and smartphones—so it's a very versatile solution. It's also one of the most powerful choices out there; and it's free! In fact, you'll see I favor ToodleDo throughout this book as the best way to quickly advance to the full MYN system. That said, I also list advanced resources Outlook users can study to take it to the next level.

Then, in Chapter 7, I show you the power of converting e-mails into tasks and how that helps you get control of your e-mail and your workday.

In Chapter 8, I show you how to take your 1MTD with you on a smartphone or tablet. This is the first chapter where I focus exclusively on ToodleDo.

Chapter 9 is an advanced chapter. There I teach you the remaining core lessons that make the 1MTD into a full MYN task list. You'll want to read and learn this if you find you are accumulating a lot of tasks in your to-do list—this chapter shows you how to master even a huge number of tasks. And by the way, while everyone can learn from Chapter 9, I show you how to *implement* the principles only in ToodleDo—again, it's the simplest, most widely usable software solution, so I favor it.

Video Version of This Book

By the way, on a few pages of the book ahead you will see links to a small number of free videos that will help you understand the concepts on the page. However, you may want to purchase a complete video version of this book that presents *all* the book material in a self-paced video class. In that class, all of the book's contents are explained graphically and important points highlighted clearly—it replaces the book and turns it into a multimedia experience! See the book's "extras" web page to view more information about both the free and paid videos.

Go to: www.1MTD.biz/extras

Let's Get Started

So, let's get started now. In the first short chapter you are going to jump right into creating your first 1MTD. Within 60 seconds, you'll have a taste of how easy and powerful this to-do list system can be.

1

60 Seconds to Workday Relief!

Learning the One Minute To-Do List (1MTD) is fast. In fact, you can learn it right now—at least at a starter level—in about 60 seconds! To get going, I'll have you take one minute to do a brain dump of things that are nagging you right now, using the 1MTD approach.

We're going to do this on paper. Find two blanks sheets of paper—either loose sheets or in a notebook. Or use the two blank pages in the book ahead. And get a pen or pencil handy.

By the way, you might be tempted to do this first exercise on a computer or mobile device—that is, type it in. If you don't mind, please hold off on that for a bit; I will show you the best ways to use a computer or mobile device in later chapters. For now, to get the one-minute experience quickly, just use a pen or pencil and some paper.

Your Critical Now List

On your first sheet of paper, or on the blank page ahead in the book, you are going to create two sections or "zones." I call these *urgency zones* and I will explain why in a later chapter.

The first urgency zone is called *Critical Now*. Write that phrase at the top left of your page: Critical Now. (That label is already on the blank page.)

Now let's make a list. List anything on your mind that you know is *absolutely due today.* Just consider what is making you nervous today. Think about what to-dos would impact you quite negatively if you did not complete them today. Write down anything that comes to mind, but don't spend more than 20 seconds on it—this is a quick brain dump. Later, you can flesh this list out a bit more.

Also keep in mind, this list may be empty; I really only want you to write tasks that absolutely must be done today. Do not write down things you'd merely *like* to do today or things that just *seem* important. No, only list things that are *absolutely due today*. If there is nothing like that, that's okay, leave it empty.

Your Opportunity Now List

Next, about one-third of the way down the page, write the heading *Opportunity Now*.

Now make a list in this section. List here those tasks that, though not urgently due now, you would work on now *if you had the opportunity.* Include things that may be due tomorrow, or later this week, or even as far out as ten days.

What do I mean by "if you had the opportunity"? Well, for example, I mean tasks you would do once your critical list was done and you had time available; having that time represents an opportunity. Or things you might do now if the right person walked by your desk and you were able to talk to them and move a task forward. Or, things you might do now if you were suddenly inspired to do them— inspiration can be an opportunity as well. All of these represent opportunities to address work even though that work is not due for up to ten days. In the next chapter I'll tell you where that ten-day cutoff comes from—why it is so meaningful.

Take 20 seconds to write those things down now. You don't need to be exhaustive—just record what first comes to mind. You can add more later. And if you think of anything that can wait longer than ten days, put it in the section I describe next.

Your Over-the-Horizon List

Finally, the third urgency zone is called the *Over-the-Horizon* zone. For this early exercise, you will create that list on your second page, either using the prelabeled page in the book ahead or your own second blank sheet of paper. If using your own paper, label it "Over-the-Horizon."

Critical Now

Opportunity Now

Over-the-Horizon

Now, write down here anything on your mind that can wait ten days or more for you to get to.

Items here are obviously your slow-burn items. These are things that are not troubling you right now as being at all urgent. But even though they are beyond your "concern horizon" (thus the term Over-the-Horizon), it is good to record them so you do not lose them; they may become more urgent later. Recording them now gives you a way to revisit them in a week or so—to check in on their fluctuating urgency.

So, do that now. Take 20 seconds and write them down. As with the previous section, there is no need to be exhaustive at this point. This exercise is just to get you started using the system; you can of course come back to this list later to make it more complete. The idea is to get whatever is *on* your mind written down, and so, *off* your mind—thus bringing you some mental relief.

What You've Just Done

Congratulations! You have just started using a very powerful, effective, and *simple* to-do list. In fact, it may seem *too* simple to you. The truth is, it is deceptively simple. But don't let the simplicity of the system fool you; this approach is incredibly powerful.

So, what have you really just done?

Well, first of all, you have probably lowered your stress level greatly. If any of those things you wrote down were previously bouncing around in your mind and causing you anxiety, you've now confidently recorded them in one compact list that you can rely on.

You can rely on the list because the first page represents all you need to worry about *today*, with the things urgently due today listed right at the top. This short list is your "concern list" for today.

You've also created a place to store slow-burn items (the second page)—items that you'd like to get recorded and off your mind.

This to-do list approach is particularly useful because it emphasizes urgency. It is urgency that causes your stress level to rise at work, and it is urgency that you should manage first. This system addresses that directly. I'll talk more about the difference between urgency and importance in the next chapter, and why this urgency approach is so powerful.

So, now that you have this three-part to-do list, update it throughout the day as new things present themselves or as priorities change. Update it as you think of things you did not recall when you started the list. For example, if you keep lists elsewhere, now is a good time to go find them and copy items into this list. You want all your needed actions listed in one place—make this that place. That includes your e-mail in-box, by the way; if you have an e-mail in there with actions due (other than a simple reply), write a one-line summary of that action in your list too.

Carry this list with you everywhere you go. Put it in your pocket or handbag; or if you carry a paper calendar journal, slip it in the front of it. You will feel the stress drain off your day as you start to realize you've got everything together now. Enjoy it!

Wrap-up

Next, I want to show you why this system works so well. The next chapter is optional, but I think you will like it.

2

Urgency Zones: The Key to Workday Control

You just saw *how* to make this to-do list; now let's see *why* this to-do list works so well. Even though it looks incredibly simple, don't be deceived—there is a deep and powerful design behind it.

And by the way, this chapter is optional—let's just say it's for people who are curious about why the list works and what the principles behind it are. I do hope you read it—I think you will find it very interesting. But if you would rather just keep moving and continue learning how to *use* the to-do list, feel free to skip to the next chapter. You can always come back to this one.

If Everything Is Important, Nothing Is

You would think using a to-do list would be easy. You simply make a list of things to do, mark their relative priority, and start working at the top of the list, right?

Wrong. Most people create and use a to-do list incorrectly—they do that because they emphasize *the wrong things.* In other words, they *prioritize* wrong. And the common reason for misprioritizing is being confused about the right way to *measure importance.* The result is that the high-priority section of the to-do list ends up being way overloaded—it displays too many items. Then, if *everything* is important, *nothing really is,* and the list becomes useless. Or, even in a short list, the wrong items get put there.

Why does this happen?

The problem is this: there is almost always some way to measure a task as being important. Here is a quick brainstorm of some different ways a task can be labeled as having high importance.

- It might be important in a timely way, i.e., urgent.
- It might be important for your career.
- It might lead in the direction of one of your important goals.
- It might match one of your important values.
- It might have a long-term impact if not attended to.
- It might be good for your health.
- It might be fun.
- It might be something you have put off a long time.
- It might be something that makes you feel guilty.
- It might be something that inspires you.
- It might be something you feel responsible for.

- It might seem morally correct.
- It might be required by someone.
- It might be important to someone you care about.
- It might be important to your boss.
- It might be important to your company.
- It might be something someone is angry about it.
- I could go on and on.

The problem is, nearly any task can be labeled important based on one of these measures. Asking yourself "Is this important?" will yield a "yes" answer to way too many tasks. So, we tend to put a lot of things in the important category—the *high* priority. And that just can't work. We cannot manage our work when all of our tasks are in the high-priority section.

And if we attempt to trim the list, it's hard to do. Which of the above criteria should rule? And then if we *force* a trim, we randomly eliminate tasks with no clear reason, and then we lose faith that the tasks remaining on the list really *do* represent what we really need to focus on. And we stop using the list.

The other thing that happens is, in the heat of the business day, when we come to things that are prioritized wrong, we just skip over them—we see they don't help reduce our anxiety about getting ahead of our current fires, so we move on to things that do. Since the list remains stuffed with things that don't get done, we give up on it.

Control Urgency to Focus on Important Work

The beauty of the One Minute To-Do List (1MTD) system is that it uses one and only one of the above criteria as a means for identifying what goes into each priority, and that's *urgency*. There is no confusion—you simply have to ask yourself the question: "Is it is absolutely, positively due today?" If "yes," then you put it in the Critical Now section. If you want it in the next week or so, it goes in the Opportunity Now section. If the answer is it can wait over ten days, it goes in the Over-the-Horizon section.

This unequivocal criterion of urgency is the main reason this to-do list is so simple and so usable. And the fact that it keeps the high-priority section from overflowing gives you faith in the list. It's also why so many people are successful with the 1MTD system—why they say it is the first to-do list system that has ever worked for them.

The result is that once you start using the 1MTD system, your urgent items will come under control, and you can now start to focus on your lower-urgency but very *important* tasks.

For example, I spend a little bit of time every morning using the 1MTD to make sure my urgent tasks are attended to. Then I take a deep breath, give a sigh of relief, and switch over to my more significant but less urgent work. It feels great because I know there is nothing that is about to unexpectedly bite me—I have all urgent items well in view and under control. In that relaxed and more creative state I can do much better work advancing my important and significant projects.

Critical Now Provides Crystal Clarity

Again, you may feel that the system seems just too simple. You may think, "It's just using three priority levels, and basing the priority on urgency; I've done that before." But in fact, there is much more to this system than that. For example, the system incorporates a number of powerful and unique rules that ensure that it works day after day. I will cover them in the next chapter.

Furthermore, while the system seems simple and almost obvious, it emphasizes some subtle but very solid principles. First of all, it's my experience, and the experience of most others, that the most common source of urgency is an impending deadline of *today*. The statement "This is absolutely due today" sets on fire almost any action request. It removes any tendency to ignore a task till later. That's why the most urgent section of the 1MTD is defined by tasks that are due today, the Critical Now section.

It's important to make that designation crystal clear and in a single list that is very visible—but most of us don't do that. Rather, most of us have urgent tasks scattered on sticky notes or buried in e-mails or in voice mails. And that's too bad, because if you're not absolutely clear about what's due today, you will lose track of urgent items and you will tend to drift over to lower-priority activities. You can then lose sight of urgent items until they are actually *overdue* and causing damage.

Having that list crystal clear greatly reduces our work-day stress, because we know exactly what we need to apply our intense and urgent focus on, and what we don't. And best of all, we know when we can relax our intense focus—when those items are done. One of the best rewards of using this system comes at the end of the day, when you look at the critical list and see it is empty. At that moment you can say to yourself, "I am done with everything urgent" and you can complete your day's work feeling relaxed and confident.

Why Ten Days?

The other brilliant thing about this system is that ten-day cutoff between the Opportunity Now zone and the Over-the-Horizon zone. It's not arbitrary; it was chosen carefully and it works very well at controlling our urgency.

So, where did that ten-day cutoff come from? It came from my years of working with and observing very busy people. I found that most people tend to relax their anxiety about a big task or project if its deadline is beyond one or two weeks out. Ask somebody if they can fit in a new half-day project in the next ten days and they'll say no. But ask them if they can get it done beyond ten days and they'll usually say yes, they can. It's not that people are any less busy beyond ten days; it's just that they emotionally relax when gazing out beyond that. It turns out that it's a very common psychological quirk we all have, and at about ten days is where it kicks in.

It's good to be aware of that quirk because it gives us a way to unload our list of highest concerns. Simply set the date of a task beyond ten days and you will suddenly relax about it. That gives us a way to limit the size of the list you *do* worry about—you'll see in a moment why that is so important.

The Opportunity Now Zone

That ten-day limit delineates the further edge of the middle list, those items in the Opportunity Now zone. Items due within one to ten days are the things you *do* want to keep your eyes on in the days ahead. While they're not absolutely due today, you'll see it's good to keep these in daily sight because they may become more urgent in the near future. And as you have time in the day to get lower priority things done, it's good to have that list at hand to pick from.

It's also a good place to put tasks that you want to think about a day or two more to decide upon their urgency; this way you can keep them in sight and consider their importance more fully. Nearly all my new tasks, if not really pressing, I put first in the Opportunity Now section. Then, later, I move many of them into the

Over-the-Horizon section as the test of time shows me that they can wait. You'll develop a natural routine of considering new tasks and triaging them into the three urgency zones—that routine, and 1MTD, keeps you well ahead of your work.

The Over-the-Horizon Zone

That ten-day limit also delineates the start of the last list, those items in the Over-the-Horizon zone. Many items just are not that urgent—they can wait quite a while, past ten days. If you know they can, you should list them in the Over-the-Horizon section. By definition, you worry much less about the items here, if at all.

In fact, while ten days is the formal lower limit for when tasks in this zone need attention, most can wait far longer than ten days. And I'll admit it—this zone is a bit of a dumping ground. It's where you put things you want to get off your Opportunity Now list, when that list is getting too long to study every day. It serves that purpose well. We'll talk more about that in the next chapter.

Wrap-up

So, as you can see, urgency zones *rock*. They are a fantastic way to get control of that thing that prevents us all from succeeding at work: out-of-control urgency. Urgency zones show us clearly what we should focus our intense concern on, and what can wait. They give us a way to immediately and unequivocally prioritize our work so that we are not overwhelmed by the chaos of "Everything is a fire" thinking. Ultimately, they clear our psyche so that we can focus quality time on our most important work while knowing that we are managing our workday just right.

Next, let's see how to manage this list so that it works day after day. I will show you a few simple rules that keep it from getting too big—these rules make sure you track your tasks with appropriate attention.

3

Rule Your To-Dos
with Ease

So far you have learned how to divide your tasks into three urgency zones and how that will help get your workday under control. With urgency under control, you can focus more time on your most important work. Ultimately, you get more of your most important tasks done.

But there are some additional rules or guidelines you now need to learn to keep your to-do list well managed. Without these rules, within a few days or weeks your list will fall prey to the same issues that cause other to-do lists to fail.

We Tend to Overload Our Lists

The first rules deal with how many tasks, maximum, you should have in each section. The number one cause of a failed to-do list, particularly those that are automated, is that the list gets too big and overwhelming.

You see, we tend to get enthusiastic about adding tasks to our list; we tend to add too many. And worse, we tend to resist throwing old tasks away once we write them down, even well after their importance has passed. Nearly everyone I know who has tried an automated task list, whether on a computer or a smartphone, has given up after three or four weeks—because the list just gets too big.

The good news is, the 1MTD is much less prone to these kinds of problems. First of all, the definition of the Critical Now section tends to keep it small and reasonably sized. Restricting it to only those tasks that have an absolute due date of today is what makes this possible.

That said, I bet within a week or two your Critical Now list is going to be quite large. Why? Because, in our enthusiasm, we tend to load up the high-priority section with tasks we feel strongly about but that are not really absolutely due. We tend to bite off more than we can chew.

Five or Fewer Critical Now Items

So, to prevent that from happening, here are two rules for the Critical Now list.

First, keep the Critical Now list to five items or fewer. If it gets larger than five items you will not get them done and something important will slip through the cracks.

How do you prevent yourself from loading more than five items in the Critical Now section? That's where the second rule comes in; it's called the *Going Home Test.* When you are about to place an item in the Critical Now section, ask yourself the following question: "Would I be willing to not go home but instead work late tonight, perhaps even till midnight or beyond, to get this item completed?" If the answer is "no," don't put it in the Critical Now list; put it in the Opportunity Now list. This stringent rule will keep your Critical Now section well controlled and easily under five items—perhaps even empty.

Twenty or Fewer Opportunity Now Items

The next rule is for the Opportunity Now list. Recall, this section represents those tasks that are not absolutely due today, but that you would like to *consider* doing today or tomorrow, or within the next ten days.

Since the items you place here are *discretionary*, this section will tend to get big, fast. Why? Because you will tend to add more items than you complete on any given day. To keep it under control, I have a simple rule for this section: limit the number of items here to 20 or fewer.

Why 20 items? Because 20 items is about the maximum number you will scan through and digest in one quick glance. You need to be able to digest this list quickly because it's the list you look to when you decide what to do when you have some nonurgent time available. Also, it might represent items that are going to be coming due relatively soon, say, in the next day or two. So if, due to its size, you don't check the list completely every day, something on that list may "pop" and lead to business issues.

That's why I say keep this list to 20 items. It's easy: if the list gets bigger than 20, just identify the lowest-priority items and move them to the Over-the-Horizon list. In this system, the Over-the-Horizon list can get as big as you want, so it becomes a catchall for things that you cannot or need not focus on in the next ten days or so. Move tasks liberally from the Opportunity Now section to the Over-the-Horizon section.

Review Cycles: One Hour, One Day, One Week

The next simple set of rules address how often to review the tasks in each of the three sections.

This is another place where this system works brilliantly. Because all your tasks are divided into urgency zones, the different urgencies allow significantly different cycles of review. This allows you to minimize your time spent inside the to-do list, limiting it to only what is absolutely needed. It's one reason this is called the One Minute To-Do List; your review of the list each day usually takes less than a minute. As a result, the to-do list is lightweight, easy to manage, and easy to keep up with. It's why people say that they succeed with this system when they have failed with others; rather than being overwhelming, the 1MTD system is actually easy to use.

Here are the simple review rules:

- Critical Now items: review approximately once each hour.
- Opportunity Now items: review approximately once each day.
- Over-the-Horizon items: review approximately once each week.

That's it! It can't get much simpler than that.

Let me explain a little why these review cycles are what they are.

First, the Critical Now items are the items that will prevent you from going home. By definition these are tasks that must be done today. So it is to your benefit to get them done early in the day. Doing so prevents a pileup of too many urgent tasks at the end of the day. Checking this list early and often ensures that you will provide adequate runway to get the urgent things done on time. It allows you, for example, to make phone calls at the optimal time of the day. It allows you to spend open time in the middle of the day to get your urgent tasks done—instead of, say, cruising e-mail and then cramming in all the urgent tasks after work hours. Checking this list hourly keeps you well ahead of your day—it keeps you laser focused.

Next, the Opportunity Now list includes items that may be due later in the week, just not now. It may include small issues that could mushroom into larger ones if you don't keep an eye on them. The most urgent tasks on the Opportunity Now list are items that may be coming due *tomorrow*. This is why I recommend you check the list at least once a day so that you can spot an impending deadline, or a mushrooming issue, and escalate it before it blows up.

Finally, the third zone—the Over-the-Horizon list—represents tasks that you do not need to worry about for ten days or longer, perhaps much longer. So it makes sense that if you check this list once every week you will catch any item that may become important within the ten-day window. This list tends to get very big over time, so you don't want to check more often than weekly or you'll become jaded with the list. Once a week is just the right review cycle for this list.

By the way, I recommend you do this review each Monday. That way, if you see any item that may become more important during the week, you can plan for it. I even recommend you put a Monday morning entry on your calendar to remind you to do this.

Write Deadlines in the Subject Line (and Use Your Calendar)

I mentioned that some tasks may have deadlines later in the week or even further out. How do you indicate the due dates for those tasks? Some automated systems allow you to set due dates that trigger alarms; we'll talk about those later in the book (Chapter 9). In the meantime, just do this: write the due date at the head of the subject line for the task. So, for example, write "DUE April 15 Submit Taxes."

This way, when you scan the Opportunity Now or Over-the-Horizon lists, you can see upcoming deadlines and keep your eye on them. When a due day arrives, move the task to the Critical Now section.

In the rare instances when a super-urgent or very important deadline is well in the future, I recommend you also make an entry on your automated calendar (I assume you have one) and set a reminder on it so that you are alerted well ahead of time. But that shouldn't happen too often.

By the way, please set due dates only for tasks that actually have deadlines. Do not succumb to older time-management recommendations to put artificial due dates on all tasks to try to trick yourself into getting them done. Doing that usually fails—we just skip the task anyway— and it often leads to larger problems. It is my experience that relatively few tasks have true, absolute deadlines; reserve due date entries only for those.

Next Actions: Write Only the Very Next Step

One last thing: I encourage you to write only *next actions* on your to-do list. What do I mean by that? I mean, don't write large, general tasks on your list like "Landscape garden" or "Performance reviews." These tasks are too big and you won't know how to start them when you see them on your list. You'll tend to skip over them and they will never get done.

Instead, identify the best very next action for each item and write that on your list. For example, instead of "Landscape garden" write "Call Jim and get name of his landscaper." Instead of "Performance reviews" write "Schedule dates of performance reviews." These items are specific steps that you can act on when you see them. Take the time to figure out what these steps are as you write down your tasks—you'll be glad you did. By the way, this concept of next actions has been around for decades, but I thank the author David Allen for highlighting their importance in his recent books.

Summary of One Minute To-Do List Rules

So, in summary, keep five or fewer items in the Critical Now list. Keep 20 or fewer items in the Opportunity Now list. And move everything else to the Over-the-Horizon list.

Review the Critical Now list approximately once each hour. Review the Opportunity Now list at least once per day. And review the Over-the-Horizon list once per week.

Do not include a deadline unless it is really needed. If needed, place the deadline date right in the subject line of the task. For crucial deadlines, consider using your automated calendar and setting an alarm on it.

Write all tasks as next actions—that is, as the next steps to take to get a larger task done.

Because these rules are so simple and so easy to remember, you'll find they lead to a very lightweight and easy-to-use system. Over and over again I hear from my readers and workshop attendees that they are grateful to finally have a simple to-do list system that really works. I think you'll find this to be true for you too. Let me share with you some of the typical experiences I hear from users.

Real-Life Experiences

Here are a few real-life stories of 1MTD users.

James

James is a busy engineer who gets far more tasks than he knows what to do with, but he has made sense out of them using 1MTD. Every morning he first checks his Critical Now list to see what things may be due today and confirms that he can get them done in his available non-meeting time that day. He then scans his Opportunity Now list and moves any items that have become critical for today to the Critical Now list. He's now done with his morning scan and can start working tasks and attending meetings.

Throughout the day, as he comes and goes from meetings, James rechecks his Critical Now list and gets some of them done. He looks for any that, due to size or complexity, may hold him back from leaving at the end of the day, and focuses on those first. He says, "That Critical Now list becomes very important to me. Once I feel the Critical Now list is under control, I can start working off the Opportunity Now list. In that latter list I look for things that feel right to do, given current priorities. I also look for things there I am *inspired* to work on." He usually gets a number of his Opportunity Now items done each day, well before they become critical. James states that without the 1MTD his work life would be miserable and chaotic.

David

David owns a small software development company. He's been using the 1MTD for years now and has his own variation for using it. He focuses almost exclusively on the Critical Now list. Each evening before he quits for the day he studies and adjusts the Critical Now list for the next day—that is his variation. That way, when he arrives in the morning, he knows exactly what he needs to work on. He tries to finish those Critical Now items before noon so that during the rest of the day he already feels ahead of the game.

Julie

Julie is an inside sales rep for a manufacturing company. She also tries to get her Critical Now items done as early in the day as possible. She says, "When I get those critical items done, or least clearly on my radar so that I know when I'm going to complete them, my whole body relaxes a bit. I just know that I've got it under control, and I can now focus on my more important efforts without fear of anything urgent blowing up on me. It's a great feeling. And before I go home I take one last look at the Critical Now list. If everything is done, and it usually is, I can leave with a clear conscience!"

Wrap-up

You now know all the rules for how to succeed with the simple 1MTD. You may have practiced a bit with it on paper and now understand how to use it. Perhaps it is already guiding your work life. With the 1MTD and these rules, you can now trust the system as something that will guide your work. You can trust it because you'll see that there is in fact a place for everything in this list and nothing gets dropped. You'll see that you have one place to look when you need to decide what to do next. This is especially key when you want to leave at a reasonable time at the end of the day; you can see whether there's anything that will prevent you from leaving. And when you leave you'll leave with a free and open heart, knowing that you have a handle on it all.

Next, let's talk about how to get your 1MTD onto your computer so you can edit it more easily and keep it in tip-top shape.

4

Simple Automated Solutions

I bet you are eager to put this to-do list in your computer or on your smartphone. Nearly all of us work on our computers much of the day, and everybody seems to be using smartphones these days, so putting the 1MTD on one or both seems like a no-brainer, right?

Well, if you've tried an automated to-do list before, I bet you have failed. Most people I know who tried have also failed. I know I was eager to use my BlackBerry task list years ago, and even the task list in Outlook seemed inviting. But I gave up quickly when using these tools. Usually what happened was the list got too big too fast, and I ended up with hundreds of tasks, most of which didn't seem appropriate to do now.

Why Automate 1MTD?

But there are huge advantages to automating your to-do list. And you are going to find that the 1MTD is very easy to automate. In fact, it was designed from the bottom up to be used in an automated fashion. Here's why you will want to do that.

The first advantage to automating the 1MTD is that you can easily move tasks between the three urgency zones you learned in Chapters 2 and 3. If you use only paper, you'll need to erase and rewrite tasks to move them. That becomes difficult once you get a lot of tasks—and the paper gets messy fast. Also, once you get over, say, a hundred or so tasks, you'll need to apply advanced 1MTD principles (shown in Chapter 9) to stay ahead. Those principles only work in task *software*—so you'll *have* to automate at that point.

The second advantage to using an automated list is that it makes it easier to copy tasks that come to you in e-mail. Today, many if not most of the action requests we get each day come to us in e-mail, and being able to easily move information from e-mail to the task list is a big time saver. Automation makes this easier.

The third reason to automate is so you can see your task list on your smartphone or tablet when traveling. When I'm at my desk I use my to-do list on my computer; but when I'm on the road I want to see that same updated list on my smartphone. I show you software ahead that enables this and syncs the two systems automatically over the air.

That brings up another point. You may be wondering whether to start using your automated to-do list on your computer, or instead just put it on your smartphone (or tablet) and work off it even when at your desk. I recommend you start with your computer and then transition a little later to adding your mobile device. That's because having it on your computer is almost always needed; most of us do much of our work on our computers. Even if you don't work predominantly on your computer, you'll find there are lots of times you want to transfer information from your computer to a listed task. As I mentioned above, this is most common with e-mail—but there are other common cases as well. For example, you'll often want to attach a computer file to your task so that it is at hand when you work on the task later.

For all these reasons you should favor having your task list on your computer first, and that's why I will start out by showing you how to automate the 1MTD there. I show mobile solutions in later chapters.

Using a Text Document as Your 1MTD

The simplest way to automate the 1MTD on your computer is to find software that allows you to create and rearrange a list; there are a lot of software packages that do that. For example, Microsoft Word works, and I will talk more about that below. Or use any other text editing software. Microsoft Excel, or any other spreadsheet software, also works. Any software that allows you to delineate three list sections will allow you to show the three urgency zones, and that is all you need for the simple versions of 1MTD.

Using a Text Document Like Word

I would start with Word. Everyone seems to own Word, especially people who work in a company that has standardized on Microsoft products. We all know how to create, save, and print a Word document. If you do not use Word, feel free to use another similar text editing software.

Figure 1. Simple text-based One Minute To-Do List

Critical Now
- call Jim about April numbers
- finish progress report
- submit expenses from Chicago trip

Opportunity Now
- get alternate quotes on Franklin job
- call Donna about meeting review
- decide on website name
- update marketing project schedule
- find someone to write user manual

Over the Horizon
- find copyeditor
- read book "The Tipping Point"

Using Word (or any text editor) to create 1MTD, you just type your tasks one per line, in three separate lists corresponding to the three urgency zones described in Chapters 2 and 3. Simply stack those three lists one above the other, adding the urgency zone headings at the top of each list (see Figure 1). Then, to rearrange the list, you simply cut and paste entries as needed.

Even better, download and use a free template that I have created for you to use in Microsoft Word, as shown in Figure 2. The template has the three

Figure 2. Microsoft Word 1MTD template

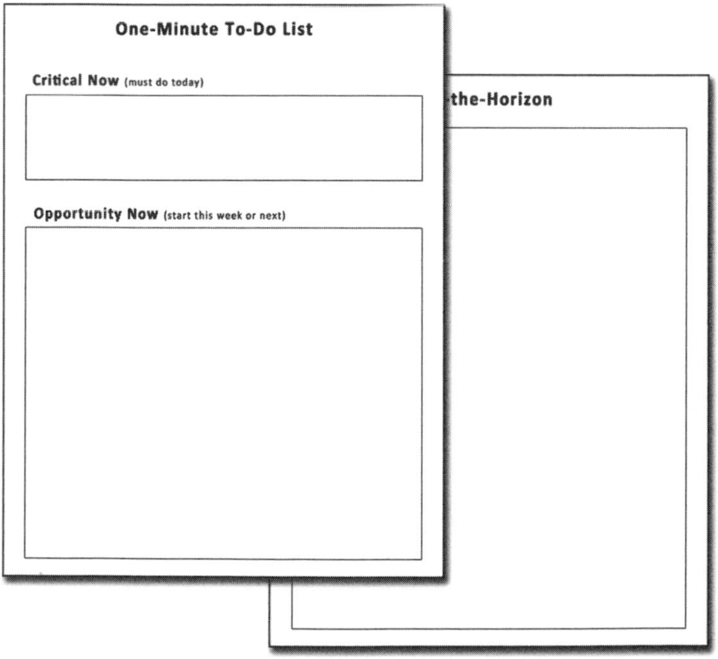

urgency zone headings locked in place, with fixed text blocks below them that you can type into. Note the Over-the-Horizon list is given its own page, since it can get rather large. You can download this at: `www.1MTD.biz/1MTD-Template.doc`

No matter what text software you use, you can leave it running on your computer screen and refer to it throughout the day. Or you can print the file and work off paper. This is handy for taking to meetings and even on the road. Throughout the day, you can make pen or pencil additions or changes right on the page. When you're back at your desk you can type the updates into your list document, save it, and then print it again for the next time you run out the door.

So yes, a simple text document can be a very easy way to start automating 1MTD, and I encourage you to try it.

Using Task Software as Your 1MTD

But you can do even better than that if you do not mind learning new software. There are a lot of applications available that are specifically designed for managing to-dos. If you look across all types of computers and mobile devices, you'll find quite a large number of titles. Some are single-purpose task applications (like ToodleDo, which I will discuss at length ahead), and others are task modules built into better-known programs (like the task module in Outlook, also discussed ahead).

I've tried or evaluated nearly all these applications and found that quite a few can be used to implement the simple principles of 1MTD—the principles you've learned so far. Really, any software that allows you to prioritize and group tasks at three levels will allow you to delineate the three urgency zones described in Chapters 2 and 3—and that's all you need if your tasks are not too numerous.

Why Use Task Software?

Dividing items into three groups may not sound very impressive, so why bother with task software at all as opposed to a text list?

The main advantage is that task software adds features—features that come in handy when your list starts to get large.

What features? First, you will want easy ways to reprioritize your tasks without needing to copy and paste—all task applications allow you to do that with a simple click. In addition, most systems also allow you to mark tasks as complete and then sort on the completed tasks for later review. Some synchronize your tasks with your smartphone.

Nearly all provide ways to set dates on tasks and then manage tasks based on those dates. For example, some software allows you to hide future tasks until their date arrives. Others have alarms on due dates.

The convenience these extra features represent is a good reason to use task software. Beyond convenience, these features become critical if you receive and accumulate a lot of new tasks each day. If you do, you'll definitely want to use one of these software solutions—they can be the only way to stay ahead of a high volume of tasks.

I Show Two Software Choices

In the chapters ahead, I am going to show you two software choices to use with 1MTD. The first is the task module built into Windows Outlook. The second is a free and simple program called ToodleDo that works on any computer.

If you do not have a lot of tasks, you can learn and successfully use either one by reading this book. That's because once you apply simple 1MTD configurations to each program (as covered in the next two chapters), they both give you the features you need to delineate and track the three urgency zones. And they both give you easy ways to move tasks between those zones.

If you *do* accumulate a lot of tasks, say, over a hundred at any given time, you'll need to use more advanced forms of 1MTD, and both programs can do that as well. However, in Chapters 8 and 9 of this book, where I teach the advanced forms of 1MTD, I am only going to show you how to use one of them, and that's ToodleDo. Why only ToodleDo? Because only ToodleDo is simple enough to show advanced levels of the 1MTD in a way brief enough for a short book like this. But even more important, since ToodleDo is very easy to learn—and since it works on PCs, Macs, tablets, and smartphones—it's the most universally usable solution of the two. I wanted to focus on a solution *every* reader can access and be successful with quickly.

In contrast, next-level Outlook training is a bit complex and requires more detailed explanations and reconfigurations than can be covered here. It also has four different active versions to explain, which takes time. And due to platform limitations, not everyone can use it or has access to it. That said, I do provide plenty of good training for Outlook users outside this book; I show you how to access that training at the end of the next chapter.

What If You Currently Use Outlook?

Are you now wondering whether to even try Windows Outlook tasks, given that the advanced part of this book ignores it? Here's my advice on that: If you are not currently using Windows Outlook for e-mail, I wouldn't transition to Outlook just so you can use its task module. Rather, use ToodleDo as shown ahead.

But if you are currently using Windows Outlook for e-mail or other purposes, here's some added advice. I'd only plan on using Outlook for *tasks* if you fit one of these two cases: 1) your task needs will remain light—you'll only track 100 or fewer tasks at any given time; or 2) your tasks needs are heavy *and* you can take one of my more advanced Outlook classes that I list at the end of the next chapter. If you fit one or both of these cases, good—proceed with Outlook. But if you do not meet either of them, I'd favor ToodleDo for tasks. Note that when using ToodleDo for tasks it's not all or nothing; you can still use Outlook for e-mail, calendar, and contacts. That's what I do and they work well together.

Also note, I consistently refer to *Windows* Outlook above. If you are using the new *Outlook 2011 for Mac,* I'd plan on using ToodleDo for tasks. There are ways to use the 1MTD in the Mac version, but they are beyond the scope of this book, even at the simple levels of 1MTD. See the third edition of my book *Total Workday Control Using Microsoft Outlook* if you really want to pursue the Mac version for tasks further.

Wrap-up

Next, I show you how to use the simple 1MTD with Outlook (Chapter 5) and then with ToodleDo (Chapter 6). Feel free to read both chapters to see which software you prefer. Or, based on my discussion above, feel free to pick one now and proceed directly to the corresponding chapter.

5

Using Outlook for the One Minute To-Do List

As I said, if you already use Windows Outlook, and your task volumes are light, you can use the tasks portion of Outlook for the simple level of 1MTD. It's easy to do that and I'll get you started here. Just know you'll have some added study, beyond this book, if you want to use Outlook for high-volume task scenarios later. I'll point you to those next steps at the end of this chapter.

Why Use Outlook Tasks

There are some advantages to using Windows Outlook for tasks if Outlook is already your main e-mail system. The number one advantage is that it's already on your desktop and you are accustomed to having it open. And with recent versions of Outlook, you can have your task list sit right next to your e-mail (using the To-Do Bar). You are more likely to use a to-do list regularly if it's constantly in plain sight like that—so this is a big plus for Outlook.

An equally important advantage is that Windows Outlook has a very quick way of converting e-mails into tasks—you just drag and drop the e-mail. Since so many of our action requests come in by e-mail these days, this is a fantastic feature. As I show in Chapter 7, converting e-mails to tasks actually helps you get control of your in-box. ToodleDo, by the way, also has a good way to do this; it's just not as smooth as Outlook's method.

And finally, many corporate IT departments, for security reasons, require that you use approved corporate software. They often want all your work data to be locked down in the server rooms of your company. If your company uses Outlook on internal servers, your IT staff will be happy that your task data is safely stored with your other Outlook data. ToodleDo's data, in contrast, is stored on outside servers—safe ones hosted by Amazon—but still outside your company's firewall.

For all these reasons, you may feel that Outlook is your choice for task management. So, let's take a look at how to use Outlook tasks for the simple 1MTD.

Getting Started with Outlook Tasks

Windows Outlook displays tasks in a number of places. If you are using one of the newer versions (Outlook 2007 or 2010), I recommend you use the task list in the To-Do Bar; that's the list on the right side of your Outlook screen.

Before you do, however, you are going to make a minor tweak to this task list to make it work better with the simple 1MTD. The tweak you are going to make is to group tasks by priority so that you can delineate the three urgency zones you learned in Chapters 2 and 3. Once you do that, the three priority levels in Outlook (High, Normal, and Low) will map to those three urgency zones.

There are three steps to make that tweak. If you already know your way around Outlook tasks, you may be able to do it just by reading the steps below. If not, I suggest you watch the online video I give a link to below—it shows you all the details.

Here are the three steps:

1. Find the task list in the To-Do Bar at the right of the screen.

2. Right-click the Arrange by (or Arranged by) label at the top of the task list (you can see that label at the top left of Figure 3).

3. Then choose Importance, as shown in the middle of Figure 3.

Then enter tasks as usual in Outlook; they'll now be displayed in urgency-zone groups as shown in Figure 4.

Outlook and 1MTD: Introductory Video

If you know Outlook tasks already and were able to follow the above-listed steps, fine. But if you are not already

Figure 3. Applying 1MTD settings to Outlook

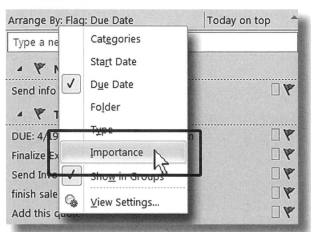

using Outlook tasks and would more clarification, that's understandable.

So instead, I am going to suggest you watch the online video I've prepared just for you. The video will not only show you how to do the tweak I listed above, but it will also get you started on using the Outlook task system—showing you how to enter tasks and use them. And even if you know and use Outlook tasks, you may want to watch this video as well—you may learn some new things. Also, at the link below I provide a free PDF e-book copy of this book—the entire book—so you can take it with you on your computer or e-reader.

Go to: `www.1MTD.biz/extras` and play Free Video #1.

By the way, this free video is a small part of the larger video class version of this course that I mentioned at the end of the Introduction. You might want to consider watching the entire video class—it replaces the book and turns it into a multimedia experience! You'll see that class described at the link above.

Using 1MTD in Outlook

Once you make the tweak to Outlook per above, your Outlook task list will look like Figure 4.

Figure 4. Outlook ready for 1MTD

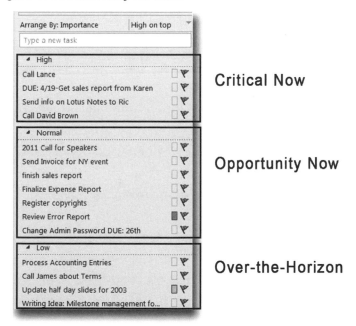

Notice the mapping to the three urgency zones? You should now use them just as you did on paper as described in Chapters 2 and 3. As you may recall, the Critical Now (or High priority) tasks are tasks absolutely due today. Opportunity Now (or Normal priority) tasks are tasks you'd like to get to in the next week or so. And Over-the-Horizon (or Low priority) tasks are tasks that can wait ten days or much longer.

Once you start entering tasks regularly, you are going to need to manage the lists so they stay at a reasonably small size. As with the paper list system, the rules to maintain the system are simple:

- Keep five or fewer items in the Critical Now list.
- Keep 20 or fewer items in the Opportunity Now list.
- Move everything else to the Over-the-Horizon list.

Nearly any task can bite you if you do not keep an eye on it; but how quickly that happens depends on which urgency zone it is in—you need to review each zone at an appropriate level of frequency. So, here is a repeat of the rules I showed for the paper list:

- Review the Critical Now list approximately once each hour.
- Review the Opportunity Now list at least once each day.
- Review the Over-the-Horizon list once each week.
- Place deadline dates right in the subject line of the tasks. For crucial deadlines, consider using your automated calendar and setting an alarm on it. You might also try

setting the Outlook task's Due Date field—it turns red
when the task is overdue—or using a task reminder; but
all that's optional. As usual, do not set deadlines unless
they are really needed.

- Finally, try to enter all tasks as next actions—small next
steps that represent the very next thing you need to do
on the task.

That's it! That is enough to get you going in Outlook.
Start entering all your tasks in Outlook today and get in
the habit of using it whenever you need to see what next
to work on.

By the way, if you want to print your Outlook task list
so you can carry it with you, there are a couple of subtle-
ties to doing that and they vary with each version of
Outlook. I have a write-up on how to do that at this link:
www.1MTD.biz/PrintCalendar.htm

Outlook Advanced Study

In a way, there are two kinds of Outlook users. There are
those who are willing to study it more extensively to take
it to the next level, and those who are not. If you are willing to study it more extensively, you can make Outlook
tasks into a very powerful task system. That's one reason
to use Outlook—it has a lot of power that can be uncov-
ered by changing its configurations.

But as I said earlier, extensive study of Outlook is
beyond the scope of this short book. So, if you want to

use Outlook and 1MTD with higher volumes of tasks, you should plan to refer to my more complete materials outside this book.

Here are your options for my more advanced Outlook study:

- You can learn my complete Outlook system by reading my book *Total Workday Control Using Microsoft Outlook* (3rd ed.). While it is much longer than this book (400 pages), it is written in a lesson format and is designed for self-study. The new edition 3 of that book covers Mac and Windows versions of Outlook from the latest version (2011) back to 2003.
- Or, you can self-study my Outlook video classes.
- Or, you can sign up for my public webinars about the MYN Windows Outlook system; this lets you learn with a group, online, using your own computer at your desk. We offer sessions three to four times a year.
- Public instructor-led classroom training on my system is available in various locations in the US.
- On-site corporate seminars can be arranged for your group or company, as can custom webinars.
- We also offer personal one-on-one instruction for those who prefer it.

Go to this link for more information on all these options: www.1MTD.biz/outlook-classes

Wrap-up

What should Outlook users do next in this book? Well, if you don't go directly to one of the advanced-study options listed above, you can still get more out of this book; you will learn next how to convert e-mails to tasks. So, at this point, Windows Outlook users, please jump to Chapter 7. You'll find that to be a valuable lesson.

6

Using ToodleDo for the One Minute To-Do List

Perhaps you do not use Windows Outlook as your e-mail system. For example, you're a Mac user who uses Mac Mail, or Entourage, or Outlook 2011 for Mac, or Gmail for your e-mail. Or perhaps you're using a Windows computer but with Gmail or some other e-mail system.

Then again, maybe you *are* using Windows Outlook but you don't want to take the time to study my more advanced Outlook training—the training I mentioned at the end of the last chapter. It does take some effort to really extract the power from Outlook tasks and I don't blame you for not wanting to jump right into that.

Or perhaps you want to use a task system that is in some ways even better than Outlook.

For these reasons and more, you need a non-Outlook system to choose from, and I recommend only one. It's a simple and universally usable software product called *ToodleDo*.

ToodleDo is amazing software. While it is a relatively new upstart in the task management world, it works better than almost any other task software out there—including Outlook tasks, in many ways. And it's free! There are paid versions (I discuss reasons to upgrade in Chapter 7), but the free version is all most people need.

Why Use ToodleDo

ToodleDo is browser based so it runs in the same easy way for all users on any computer or tablet (Windows, Mac, Linux, iPad, Android, and so on). That means *anyone* can use it, no matter what hardware they use.

Not only is ToodleDo browser based, but the browser version is its *main* version—it was designed from the ground up to be used primarily in a browser. That's in contrast to many other programs where a browser version is supplied as a scaled-back "lite" implementation. (Outlook's OWA is an example, and for that reason it is not usable for more advanced 1MTD tasks.)

And the browser version of ToodleDo works really well. That's because the makers of ToodleDo have done an especially good job at implementing its browser *controls*. This is a fine point but it's worth mentioning. We've all seen browser-based interfaces that are painful to use compared to dedicated applications; command buttons and drop-down fields are clumsy and slow to use. Or you have to wait for a full refresh every time you make small changes. But that's not the case with ToodleDo. Its controls are really well designed, quick, and even a pleasure to use—even on smaller screens like those on a tablet.

But what about the *tiny* windows on some smartphones where browser software is difficult to use? Well, ToodleDo also has apps that run on nearly every smartphone—so you are covered there as well.

Preconfigured Advanced 1MTD In ToodleDo

There is one more reason I've picked ToodleDo as the task software I recommend you use with this book. ToodleDo is very easy to use with my more advanced 1MTD teachings. Why? Because, at my request, the makers of ToodleDo have created a preconfigured version of ToodleDo that implements the advanced 1MTD principles called MYN—the ones you will learn in Chapter 9. If you are getting lots of new tasks each day, you'll definitely want to learn and use the MYN principles. So, when you get to that chapter, there's no extra work for you to do—with one click you can activate all the MYN settings in ToodleDo and be ready to go. By the way, Outlook users don't have this instant setting ability. Rather, I spend almost 20 pages in my Outlook books showing users how to make MYN settings—they are much harder to make there; so, be thankful that ToodleDo has these instant settings!

You Can Use It with Any E-mail System

And finally, even if you use Outlook or another system for e-mail, you can still use ToodleDo for your tasks—ToodleDo can be used together with *any* e-mail system. That's what I do—I use ToodleDo for tasks and Outlook for everything else, and they work great together. The reason ToodleDo works with any e-mail system is that it has a flexible way of converting e-mails to tasks. You can use it with Gmail, Yahoo, Lotus Notes, and so on. More on all that in Chapter 7.

Getting Started with ToodleDo

All right, it's time now to start using ToodleDo and learning how to use it with 1MTD. For this chapter, I am going to focus on *simple* uses of 1MTD with ToodleDo; it's the best way to learn. It's also a good foundation for later chapters where I'll up the ante a bit and show you more powerful principles of task management and how to do them in ToodleDo.

ToodleDo and 1MTD: Introductory Video

Even though ToodleDo is easy use, you do need to learn how to use it. While I could write out all the ToodleDo steps here in the book, I think a video is a much better learning experience. So, I have created an introductory video just for book readers. Since nearly all of us are always online these days, this should be easy for you to do right now; get your browser ready.

In this video you will see an overview of ToodleDo, how to get started using it, and how to enter tasks. I'll also show you how to make a few quick tweaks in ToodleDo to make it work better with 1MTD. The video is only about ten minutes long and is simple to follow. Try it now—I think you'll like it. The link appears below. At this link I also provide a free PDF e-book copy of this book— the entire book—so you can take it with you on your computer or e-reader.

Go to: www.1MTD.biz/extras and play Free Video #2

By the way, this free video is a small part of the larger video class version of this course that I mentioned at the end of the Introduction. You might want to consider watching the entire video class—it replaces the book and turns it into a multimedia experience! See the link above for more information.

Using 1MTD in ToodleDo

At this point you've watched the video on ToodleDo, and made the tweaks I recommend there. The left side of your ToodleDo screen should now look like Figure 5, with tasks grouped by Priority.

Notice in Figure 5 how we are mapping ToodleDo Priorities to the three urgency zones? Use them just as

Figure 5. ToodleDo ready for 1MTD

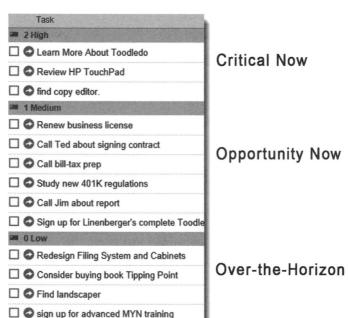

you did in Chapters 2 and 3 for paper tasks. Here's a brief review to remind you of the principles:

The Critical Now (or High priority) tasks are tasks absolutely due today. Opportunity Now (or Medium priority) tasks are tasks you'd like to get to in the next week or so. And Over-the-Horizon (or Low priority) tasks are tasks that can wait approximately ten days or much longer.

Once you start entering tasks regularly, you are going to need to manage the lists so they stay at a reasonably

small size. As with the paper list system, the rules to maintain the system are simple:
- Keep five or fewer items in the Critical Now list.
- Keep 20 or fewer items in the Opportunity Now list.
- Move everything else to the Over-the-Horizon list.

Nearly any task can bite you if you do not keep an eye on it; but how quickly that happens depends on which urgency zone it is in—you need to review each zone at an appropriate level of frequency. So, here is a repeat of the rules I showed for the paper list:
- Review the Critical Now list approximately once each hour.
- Review the Opportunity Now list at least once each day.
- Review the Over-the-Horizon list once each week.

You might be tempted to use the Due Date field in ToodleDo, and you can if you want. But, as with the paper system, I recommend you place the deadline date right in front of the subject line of the task; for example, "DUE April 15 Mail in Taxes." And for crucial deadlines, consider using your automated calendar and setting an alarm or reminder on it—we are all trained well to notice calendar deadlines. However, only set a deadline if it is really needed—don't use artificial deadlines; they never work. I talk more about using deadlines in ToodleDo in Chapter 9.

Finally, try to enter all tasks as next actions—small next steps that represent the very next thing you need to do on the task.

Wrap-up

That's it! That is enough to get you going in ToodleDo. Start using ToodleDo now as a place to keep all your tasks. I'll show you a bit more in later chapters. And if you want to take ToodleDo to the next level with detailed training now, consider our "Full" ToodleDo class listed on the book "extras" page: www.1MTD.biz/extras

Next, I want to show you how to convert e-mails to tasks. Doing so can make a very significant positive impact on your workday.

7

Controlling E-mail with the One Minute To-Do List

You may wonder why we have a chapter about e-mail in a to-do list book. Here's why: out-of-control e-mails lead to dropped responsibilities—dropped to-dos. E-mail is a major receiving area for the many new to-dos we get each day. So, if we cannot manage our e-mail, we cannot manage our tasks.

This is pretty common. Many people say their in-box is out of control—it's overloaded with older e-mails they still need to attend to, and those drag down their day. I feel that the e-mail management problem is really a *task* management problem. In other words, the reason our in-boxes are so large and out of control is because tasks in the e-mail are out of control. Let's talk more about that.

While we don't realize we're doing it, most of us are trying to use our in-box as a task management system. But doing that leads to problems. For example, when you leave e-mails with pending tasks in your in-box with the intention to act on them later, you have to constantly rehash old mail looking for those to-dos. And since the subject line of the e-mail rarely matches the action request inside, you need to reread a lot of your mail, often multiple times, to find things. It's incredibly inefficient and a big waste of time—the in-box is a lousy task manager!

The core problem is that the e-mail in-box does not have the tools to manage tasks. For example, you cannot easily change the subject of these e-mails to an action phrase. You cannot easily prioritize them in the in-box. And you cannot easily schedule them for action. You *can* do all these things, easily, in a good task management system.

As a result of trying to manage tasks in the in-box, the in-box becomes overcrowded and out of control. Since one out of five or ten e-mails sitting in your in-box represents a task to do, you are afraid to throw anything away or file them away in bulk. No wonder the in-box gets huge.

In contrast, a good task management system like 1MTD can serve as a way to solve your overloaded in-box. In fact, in my seminars on task management, I teach people how to empty their in-boxes every day. It's not that hard to do once you have a good task system in place.

The solution is to convert action e-mails into tasks and manage them where tasks should be managed: in your to-do list system. In Outlook and ToodleDo it is actually easy to convert e-mails to tasks; doing so only takes a few seconds. I'll show you how to do that in a moment.

Once you do start converting action e-mails to tasks, the tension is removed from your in-box because all the responsibilities have been transferred into your to-do list where they can be properly managed. At that point, it is very easy to empty your in-box; the mail that's left in there is merely informational and easy to file away.

And once you start converting e-mails to tasks, you'll find that you get through your e-mail much more quickly. Why? Because you are no longer bogged down by trying to work tasks in your e-mail as you see them. Often you work nonurgent e-mail requests the moment you see them just because you are afraid you'll lose them later. That causes you to get stuck in your in-box for hours processing new mail.

So, rather than spending ten to 20 minutes working on one e-mail task just because it is right in front of you, use the 1MTD to convert it into a prioritized task in just a few seconds and move on to the next e-mail. This allows you to get through your new day's worth of e-mail in one quick sitting. Perhaps for the first time in your professional career you'll be quickly speeding through your in-box. Then you can address your work in a prioritized fashion by working off your prioritized to-do list. What a concept—working your most important tasks first! That is what converting e-mails to tasks allows.

How to Convert E-mails to Tasks

So, how do you convert e-mails to tasks? It's easy, but it depends on what software you are using.

If You Are Using Outlook

In Outlook you simply drag the e-mail to the tasks icon on the left side of the screen. When you do that, a new task window pops up that is prepopulated. The title of the task is the same as the title of the e-mail; the body of the task contains the body of the e-mail. All you need to do is to type over the title to create a very clear action phrase, then set a priority and click Save. With that, you are done. It takes only a couple of seconds.

Having the body of the task contain the body of the e-mail is incredibly useful. That's because at the time you work the task you do not even need to look for the original e-mail to review the context; it's all right there in the task. And there are easy ways to pick up any attachments in the e-mail and include them in the task as well. To see how this works, watch the following short video.

Go to: www.1MTD.biz/extras and play Free Video #3.

If You Are Using ToodleDo

ToodleDo has a very easy mechanism to convert e-mails from any e-mail system into ToodleDo tasks. It works with systems like Gmail, Yahoo, Hotmail, Lotus Notes, and so on. And of course it works with Outlook e-mail as well.

You might wonder how you use a separate e-mail system to communicate with ToodleDo. It's easy. All you do is *forward* the e-mail to a specific address that ToodleDo associates with your account, and the e-mail is automatically entered into your ToodleDo server as a task. It takes seconds.

For example, let's say I get an e-mail in Outlook that I know I need to convert into a task in ToodleDo. I simply click Forward on my Outlook e-mail system, select a ToodleDo address that I earlier entered in my Outlook address book (with AutoFill, it pops in after a few keystrokes), type over the forwarded e-mail subject line to create an action phrase, and click Send. Within seconds, the e-mail appears as a task in my ToodleDo task list. And with the paid premium version of ToodleDo, attachments in the e-mail are transferred as attachments in the resulting tasks. (This is the main reason to consider purchasing the premium version of ToodleDo.) To see how all this works, watch the following short video.

Go to: www.1MTD.biz/extras and play Free Video #4.

Start Converting E-mails to Tasks Today

I cannot emphasize enough how powerful converting e-mails to tasks is. Following the simple steps above, you now have a way to get control of tasks that are clogging up your in-box. Start doing this right away.

Single-Folder Filing

By the way, once you start converting e-mails to tasks, you will find it is very easy to file mail out of your in-box. That's because the tension has been removed from the in-box. There's no need to refer to the in-box when looking for actions—they are now in your to-do list.

So, now that filing is easier, how should you file your mail? In my live classes and programs I spend a lot of time on e-mail control, and the main solution I teach is single-folder filing. You see, most people who file their mail file it into 10, 20, or 30 different topic-named folders, but still lose control of their e-mail. They think that multiple folders will help them get organized and help them find mail more easily. But in reality, that approach tends to be too complicated; it is slower for filing and slower for finding mail. Because it is so slow for filing, people often go weeks or months before filing their mail, and then they don't know where to look for it.

Instead, I teach a procedure of dragging all e-mail to *one* folder, and emptying the in-box every day. In Outlook and in other folder-based e-mail applications, I have users create a new folder called the Processed Mail folder. In an application like Gmail, I just have them use their Archive space. They file *all* their mail in the single location (except for junk, which they delete).

How is this possible? Well, once you extract tasks from e-mail as I teach above, it is very easy to do this filing and actually empty your in-box each day. Once you extract and create tasks, there's nothing left hanging in the in-box that you feel you need to act on. So it is easy to file it—you just move it all into one folder.

And when you want to find the mail later, I emphasize that people should use the indexed search engines that are built in to nearly all good e-mail software these days. Nearly all mail can be found almost instantly using these new powerful search engines. And with a single folder, it is also easy to sort on the sender column and then do a visual scan of all mail from an individual. Or you can sort on the date column and do a visual search of mail chronologically. Many of us do both of these sorts now in our overflowing in-box; it's better to just draw the line between new, unread mail and older, completed mail by doing all of it in a single filing location.

Now, all that said, some people truly do need topic filing. An example would be an attorney who needs to group mail by client and perhaps hand the whole collection off to another attorney. So, in cases like that, I advise people to use *tags* on their mail in that single folder and then group by those tags when they need to. Outlook uses Outlook *Categories* as tags—this feature has been in place in Outlook for years. It works well and is very easy to use. I show you how in my more advanced training, listed at the end of Chapter 5. In Gmail you use a feature called *Labels* to tag mail. In either system, once mail is tagged, it's very easy to trigger a view where mail appears in folder-like groups based on those tags. For example, see Figure 6 to view how this looks in Outlook.

Figure 6. Folder-like groups of mail by tagging; Outlook example

Copy All Tasks into Your 1MTD

By the way, e-mail isn't your only source of tasks—tasks can come to you from many sources. But no matter where they come from, I encourage you to use the 1MTD as your one place to list them. A lot of power comes from having one list of tasks. With one list you know what your next task is—there never is any doubt. And what's especially useful is that when you're ready to leave at the end of the day you can quickly see, at one glance, if you can leave without dropping any important tasks.

Committing to a single place to store tasks means that if tasks appear in your voicemail you make a notation for each one in your to-do list. If you have tasks that you jotted down in paper meeting notes or on slips of papers from phone calls or even from hallway conversations, immediately place all those tasks in your list so you can track them together. You'll be glad you did!

Wrap-up

Once you have 1MTD in place, I encourage you to start converting action e-mails to tasks. It will help get your in-box under control and keep you from dropping responsibilities. Once action e-mails are converted to tasks, you stop scanning through old mail, over and over, looking for things you think you still need to do—those are now converted to prioritized tasks.

Then I encourage you to consider using the single-folder form of filing mail so that you can empty your in-box every day. Emptying your in-box daily removes a ton of stress—it just feels great! And it makes you more efficient because you make a clear decision each day about what mail you are done with. It helps you make a clear distinction between new and old mail. You will reread and rehash mail much less often and end up with more time in your day.

Next, I will show you how to take your 1MTD mobile on your smartphone or tablet.

8

Going Mobile: Using 1MTD on Your Smartphone or Tablet

Smartphones are ubiquitous these days and they can do a lot of things that our computers do. So, when you are away from your computer, it seems a shame not to use your smartphone for your task list as well.

Or maybe you have one of the new tablets like the iPad or Android. These tablets are innovative and practical and can even take the place of our computers—many people are using tablets instead of laptops when working on the road. So, it makes sense to find ways to implement your 1MTD system on them as well.

Going Mobile

The reasons for putting your 1MTD on your mobile devices are obvious. You might be working away from the office and don't have your computer with you. Or you do have your computer but you don't want to take the time to open it just to take a quick glance at your tasks. Or you might have some time while in a waiting area and want to see the most urgent tasks on your list, just in case something is coming due. Or perhaps one of your tasks is to buy some groceries and you need to see the list while in the grocery store. All of these scenarios beg for a mobile task list.

However, while the reasons for going mobile with your 1MTD are obvious, how to actually take tasks mobile is not as obvious. Choosing software that works with the 1MTD and syncing tasks with your computer are the main barriers here.

So, in this section I show you how to activate your 1MTD on a smartphone or tablet. I tell you what software to use on what device. I guide you in how to set it up so it matches 1MTD principles. And I reveal how to configure it so that it syncs with your computer-based tasks—something that is important to do and often very difficult.

By the way, as I mentioned earlier, you may be tempted to just run your entire to-do list off your smartphone or tablet and not even have the task list on your computer. But as I stated before, I think that's not the right way to go. Why? Because there are a number of tasks related to your to-do list that you will want to do while working at your computer. The main example is e-mail. As e-mail comes in while you are working on your computer, you'll want to copy some of your mail to your to-do list; that's something much easier to do on your computer than on your smartphone. So, no—I'd plan to keep tasks active in both places.

Keeping Tasks in Sync

Of course, that means you'll want to keep the to-do lists on multiple devices in sync. Synchronizing data between computers and mobile devices can be challenging; it's nearly always the major source of complaints about mobile devices in the business world. That's why you want to make sure you use a to-do list software system that is designed from the outset to synchronize.

Not too long ago the standard way to synchronize with a mobile device was to plug it into the computer and run a synchronization program. However, while that may work for music or photos, that's not the way to go for rapidly changing business data like e-mail, calendar, contacts, *and tasks*. I feel strongly that data like that, including tasks, should sync over the air, automatically, in the background, and always be up to date. I very specifically include tasks in that list because once you start relying on your task list, you'll see that you really do need a task list that is always up to date. Here's one example of why: if near the end of the day you convert an e-mail to a Critical Now task (meaning it's due that day) and you run off to an end-of-day meeting, that task had better be there on your mobile device minutes later so that you are reminded to complete it before you leave work for the day. Tasks can move fast in today's world.

Putting Your Tasks in "the Cloud"

For this reason, I think it's important that you keep your tasks in *"the cloud."* This term refers to having data on a server that you can access over the Internet. And in this case it means being able to access it that way from your mobile device.

Outlook with Exchange Server allows you to do this. Setting this up, however, is difficult to do and well beyond the scope of this book. To learn how to do this for Outlook and Exchange, see the advanced training listed at the end of Lesson 5.

In contrast, ToodleDo is much easier to go mobile with and *can* be covered in the remainder of this book; we'll do that next.

Note: This is the point in the book where we fully leave Outlook behind and focus solely on ToodleDo—I warned you earlier that would happen! Of course any of you can read on from here. But if you want to do the exercises, then I assume you are using ToodleDo as your task system.

Going Mobile with ToodleDo

ToodleDo is true "server" software in every sense of the word. It serves tasks to your computer, and it serves your tasks to as many mobile devices as you choose to use. It works with all brands of smartphones, tablets, laptops, netbooks, and so on. It stores your tasks centrally in the cloud, which means you can get at your tasks from anywhere that you can access the Internet. And your tasks are automatically backed up for you by the ToodleDo company.

Technical Note: ToodleDo uses Amazon's highly reliable server farm for all its storage, as do many well-known cloud-based services like Dropbox, Zmanda, and Ubuntu. So, you can trust that your data is well supported.

Browser Based and App Based

One of the especially nice features of ToodleDo is that its browser-based version, the one you are using with ToodleDo now on your computer, is extremely flexible and so can be used on large-screen mobile devices like tablets. You can even run ToodleDo on the browsers of large-screen smartphones. (I recommend a screen size of four inches or larger to do that, and note that add-on browsers sometimes work better than native ones.)

However, on smartphones with *small* screens, controls in a browser window will be difficult to manipulate. So, another great feature of ToodleDo is that it runs in a wide variety of dedicated apps that are all optimized for small smartphone screens. And with those apps you can use ToodleDo even offline—when the Internet is not available—say, on a plane. You can't do that with a browser-based application.

The number and range of mobile apps that work with ToodleDo is amazing. On the iPhone and iPad, the ToodleDo company has created its own apps and they work great. For other platforms like Android, WebOS, and BlackBerry, the ToodleDo company has not supplied apps, but third-party companies have—and they all interface with the ToodleDo servers.

Let's go over the list of apps below and show which platforms each one works with; you will likely be choosing one or more of these. In all cases, I favor apps that can be used for both the simple 1MTD principles (those shown so far in this book) and the advanced forms of 1MTD (what I teach in the next chapter).

iPhone and iPad

On the iPhone and iPad, the app to choose is called ToodleDo (note, there are separate iPhone and iPad versions). These apps have been created by the ToodleDo company and so match the ToodleDo browser-based functionality well.

I have a video showing how to install, configure, and use the ToodleDo iPhone and iPad apps. Please go to this link to see this video; it will show you all you need to know.

Go to: www.1MTD.biz/extras and play Free Video #5.

Android

Android has a number of third-party apps that interface with ToodleDo, but as of this writing only one worked with the full range of 1MTD settings. It's called Pocket Informant Android, and it includes both a task and a calendar app—the tasks portion syncs with ToodleDo servers. I have video-based instructions for installing, configuring, and using Pocket Informant Android for 1MTD; that video is at the following link.

Go to: www.1MTD.biz/extras and play Free Video #6.

BlackBerry

As of this writing a BlackBerry option was just being finalized that fits our needs. It's a third-party app called Pocket Informant BlackBerry—by the same makers as the Android app I just described above. As with the Android app it syncs with ToodleDo's servers. It should be available on BlackBerry App World by the time you read this. And I will post a video showing how to install, configure, and use the app at the following link.

Go to: www.1MTD.biz/extras and play Free Video #7.

Other Smartphones, Tablets, and Software

There are a number of less popular smartphone and tablet choices available—ones that currently hold little market share. New software choices are often coming out for these and the main platforms; many may support 1MTD. See the following link for my Software web page, which I keep up to date as new apps emerge.

Go to: www.1MTD.biz/Software.html

Wrap-up

So, that is the overview of your mobile solutions for 1MTD. As you can see, your choices on the three major smartphone and tablet platforms are robust and usable. In no time at all you should have your ToodleDo-based 1MTD running on your smartphone or tablet.

Next, I'm going to show you how to take 1MTD to the next level. This is optional but recommended because it adds a number of useful features and capabilities that you may like—and they are features you will need if your task list gets long. At this next level, the system is called Master Your Now! or MYN for short. It's not for everyone—it involves a little extra work—but check it out to see if it's something you can benefit from.

9

Taking 1MTD to the Next Level

Congratulations—you have finished the bulk of your to-do list training! You have completed the core steps of what I consider to be the best to-do list management system in the world. By using it, you are now starting to get your tasks under control. But soon, if not now, you will want to take 1MTD to the next level. You'll want to up the ante and learn some advanced processes.

When is a next level really needed? If you've accumulated over 100 tasks, it's probably time to advance to the next level. Things start to get complicated once you are tracking a lot of tasks. It's hard to scan a very big list. Even with 1MTD rules, you'll start to lose faith that you are tracking all tasks appropriately. And the time it takes to manage that many tasks can prevent you from doing it properly.

So, you'll want to extend 1MTD a bit, and this next level of the 1MTD does that—it makes managing a lot of tasks easy.

The Next Level Is Called "MYN"

I have a specific name for this next level: I call it *Master Your Now!* or MYN for short. MYN is the complete task system I have been teaching for years. I wrote about MYN in two earlier books, *Master Your Workday Now!* and *Total Workday Control Using Microsoft Outlook;* but those are long books and not for quick review. So, in this chapter, I show you how to use MYN in a much simpler and quicker way. You'll be up and running with it in no time—without having to commit to many hours of study.

What's in MYN?

MYN helps you manage high volumes of tasks. One of the first places you're going to accumulate too many tasks is in your Opportunity Now list. When that gets too long, you'll need to prioritize within the list. To that end, MYN includes a concept called *FRESH Prioritization*—it provides a natural approach to managing a long list of tasks in your Opportunity Now section. You'll learn how to use that ahead.

I'll also show you the important MYN concept called *Defer-to-Do,* which shows you how to schedule tasks for when you want to work on them. That hides tasks until they are really needed, which helps keep your list shorter and more focused.

Both these concepts rely on using *start dates* on all tasks; using start dates effectively is one of the unique approaches of the MYN system. So, we'll talk a lot about the value and importance of using start dates on tasks.

Two other concepts from MYN are covered ahead: *Significant Outcomes* and *Defer-to-Review.* The former helps manage larger, more important tasks; and the latter is useful for managing too many Over-the-Horizon tasks.

ToodleDo Implementation

For all these concepts, I'll show you how to implement them in ToodleDo. Thanks to ToodleDo's simplicity, you'll find this is quite easy. In fact, the makers of ToodleDo have provided a one-step settings change that implements all the MYN settings at once. I'll show you that in this chapter.

If you're using Outlook, you can of course read this chapter as well, but I won't show you here how to implement the principles in Outlook. As discussed in Chapter 5, doing this in Outlook is beyond the scope of a short book like this; there are just too many steps and too many variations across Outlook versions. If you are committed to using Outlook, I encourage you to use the resources that I've listed at the end of Chapter 5. Everything I cover here (and much more) is applied to Outlook in those options. Any one of those resources will teach you the full Outlook-based MYN system.

So, ToodleDo users, let's get started on these more advanced 1MTD concepts—the MYN principles. I think

you will find they make your busy workday much easier
to master.

FRESH Prioritization

Now that you've been using the system a bit, have you
noticed that your Opportunity Now section is getting big?
Have you thought to yourself, "Wow, there are a lot of
tasks here. Shouldn't I list important ones at the top? How
do I do that?" FRESH Prioritization is a simple and natural
answer. You implement it by using start dates on all your
tasks and sorting them a certain way. It is very simple to
do, and it's an important new principle of automated task
management.

What Is FRESH Prioritization?

If you've ever used a paper-tasks approach in which you
create a new page for each day, you'll recognize exactly
what this is and why it's valuable.

In most paper calendar and to-do journals, you start a
new page for each day. Then, throughout the day, as new
tasks come in, you put them on that new page. Think
about the implications of doing this: you're emphasizing
new tasks over older tasks that may be listed in previous
pages of your journal. In other words, you've made sure
the newer tasks get more attention by putting them on
today's page.

Of course, when you started the new page for the day,
you may have glanced back to your previous pages to see

if there were any to-dos that had not yet been completed. And if you found some that were really important, you may have copied those forward to the new page. But the less important, uncompleted tasks you probably left on the older pages knowing that you could always flip back and find those if you needed to.

This is what FRESH Prioritization does. It's based on that same paper-based experience where newer tasks warrant more attention, and older ones less, unless you promote specific older ones. And I bet that intuitively felt correct to you. That's because the priorities of your company, your boss, and you *do* in fact often change quickly over time. And the newer tasks you write down *do* tend to represent the latest priorities. Because of this process, these paper systems were in a way *self-cleaning*—as you turned the pages only tasks with newer priorities stayed in the forefront; the older, deader tasks fell out of sight.

What I call FRESH Prioritization is just the computer equivalent of doing that. It's a way of managing a computerized list of tasks that imitates that convenient behavior of those older paper systems.

This can be done easily in any computerized to-do list that has any kind of date field—but it's best done using the *Start* Date field. In ToodleDo, we simply make sure *all* tasks have a start date assigned. And we set a ToodleDo default such that today's date is automatically inserted in the Start Date field of all new tasks. You then set the sorting such that tasks with newer start dates sort to the top. And that's it—that's all it takes to implement FRESH Prioritization. With this approach, the tasks you see first at the top of your Opportunity Now list are probably going to be ones with the most energy and most freshness. They tend to be your most important optional tasks.

And by the way, FRESH is an acronym that stands for Fresh Requests Earn Sorting Higher; it's a statement of the underlying principle.

Some Older Tasks Are Still Important

Now, not all tasks lose importance over time. So, if you look lower in your Opportunity Now list and see some tasks that are still very important and they seem positioned too low, all you need to do is set the start date of those to a more recent date (today, yesterday, or a few days ago), and that will move those tasks up higher in your list. This allows you to reprioritize on the fly. Don't set them to the future, though—I discuss why in the next section.

If the discussion above left you a bit confused, no worries; in the video I link ahead, I'll demonstrate all these principles with examples. So, you'll "get" it in the video.

This system of sorting to implement FRESH Prioritization helps keep your task list fresh and more usable. In fact it's exactly opposite to how most other task systems work with their default configurations. For example, out-of-the-box Outlook sorts the oldest incomplete tasks to the top of the list. It then turns them bright red to suggest that these are the ones you should do first. This is based on 50-year-old principles of task management that I feel just do not work anymore. And that's why I think most people give up on most automated task management systems—because they highlight old, dead tasks. Such systems don't feel right and we get frustrated and give up on them.

So, start paying attention to the start dates in your tasks. Once you turn on the MYN settings in ToodleDo (discussed next), start dates and FRESH Prioritization will be set automatically. You'll soon be changing the start dates as needed to sort your list appropriately.

Don't Use a Due Date, Use a Start Date!

The concept of using a start date brings up another important new principle of task management. That's to favor start dates on all tasks, rather than due dates, when scheduling tasks.

What do I mean by that?

You've probably heard the maxim "If you don't set a due date on something it won't get done." This principle sounds very proactive. It is the reason nearly all task management software programs have a Due Date field on their tasks. Nearly all paper task lists also show a Due Date space for you to write in.

But setting a due date for all tasks is another one of those old principles that sound good but don't in fact work.

Why doesn't it work? Because you're trying to trick yourself and you aren't that easily tricked. It's like the person who sets his wristwatch ahead ten minutes thinking he'll be on time for all meetings from then on. But after a few days he mentally adjusts to the time change and starts being late again. It's the same with artificial due dates; if you set a date that's fake you'll know it's fake and you'll ignore it. In fact you may miss some important deadlines because you'll get in the habit of ignoring all due dates you write down.

So, don't write a due date on a task unless there truly is a deadline for that task. I'll review some of the rules that I have for setting deadlines on tasks in a moment.

Set Start Dates on All Tasks

While I want you to ignore the old "always use a due date" rule, here is an important corresponding MYN rule that I *do* want you to follow: set a start date on *all* your tasks. Why? A start date in MYN plays two very important roles. The first role is what we just described above: a way to control FRESH Prioritization. For example, if you want to see a task at the top of your Opportunity Now list, set the start date to today. And if you have a new task that is not very important and you want to see it listed below

your other tasks, set the start date to an older date, further
in the past—that will cause it to drop down in your list.
Again, this is FRESH Prioritization at work.

But the other role of the start date comes into play
when you begin setting start dates to the *future*. Doing
that allows you to *schedule when tasks will appear on
your list.*

Essentially, what the future start date tells you is this:
when you want to first *see* the task or when you want
to *start thinking about doing* the task. When you make
future settings in ToodleDo, a future-dated task will be hidden until the start date arrives. So, in essence, this is not a
due date but rather it is a *"do"* date. It's the day you want
to start thinking about *doing* the task. Tasks postponed to
a future date like this I call *Defer-to-Do* tasks.

When you've got a lot of tasks on your list, using Defer-
to-Do tasks is a good way to shorten your list—it allows
you to hide tasks you don't need to think about right now.

Again, in the video ahead, I'll demonstrate all these
principles; so if the discussion above left you a bit confused, you'll understand it once you watch the video.

In ToodleDo, you need to make one configuration
change to enable Defer-to-Do tasks. You can do
that change manually or you can activate it automatically
as part of the preconfiguration setting I will show you
next. In fact, this is a good reason to turn on those preconfigurations now; so let's do that next.

Turning on ToodleDo MYN Preconfigurations

Now that you have worked your way through various introductory levels of 1MTD, let's turn on the full MYN settings for ToodleDo. This will activate the Start Date field and the capability to hide tasks with future start dates—two things that meet our immediate needs.

But turning on the full MYN settings for ToodleDo also does a lot more. Here's a complete list of all the changes turning on these settings makes and how it helps you manage your workday in ToodleDo.

- As mentioned, it activates the Start Date field, which you'll need to use for all tasks.
- It moves the Priority column over to the leftmost position, since it's your most important field.
- It sets the sorting on Priority ascending first, and then Start Date *descending* within each Priority group. This enables urgency-zone sorting and FRESH Prioritization within the Opportunity Now group.
- It activates default values for all new tasks as follows: start date is set to Today and priority is set to Medium; these defaults make sense for the MYN system.
- It adds the Trashcan column to allow you to delete tasks more easily.
- It adds a number of other sort settings to less used views.

Again, you could make all these settings one at a time by hand in ToodleDo, but the easiest way to go is to activate the MYN preconfigurations. And the best way to show you where to click to activate these preconfigurations is to show you a video. So, at this point, please watch the video at the link I show below. This video also shows you some tips for using ToodleDo with the new MYN settings.

Go to: www.1MTD.biz/extras and play Free Video #8.

In fact, you may want to watch that video a few times to really "get" all the new power you have with the MYN settings.

By the way, Outlook users don't have this instant-setting ability. Rather, Outlook users have to make all

Figure 7. ToodleDo with MYN configurations

Priority ▲	Task	Start Date	Due Date	Repeat		
2 High						
☐ 2 High	Review HP TouchPad	Jul 05	no date	None		
☐ 2 High	Learn More About Toodledo	Jul 04	Aug 02	Weekly		
☐ 2 High	find copy editor.	Jun 26	no date	None		
1 Medium						
☐ 1 Medium	quick task	Today	no date	None		
☐ 1 Medium	Call Bill-tax prep	Jul 08	Aug 02	None		
☐ 1 Medium	Sign up for Linenberger's complete ToodleDo 1MTD vide...	Jul 01	no date	None		
☐ 1 Medium	Study new 401K regulations	Jun 30	no date	None		
☐ 1 Medium	Renew business license	Jun 27	Aug 01	None		
☐ 1 Medium	Call Jim about report	Jun 21	no date	None		
0 Low						
☐ 0 Low	New Low Priority Task	Today	no date	None		
☐ 0 Low	Find landscaper	Jul 14	no date	None		
☐ 0 Low	Consider buying book Tipping Point	Jul 06	no date	None		
☐ 0 Low	Redesign Filing System and Cabinets	Jun 27	no date	None		
☐ 0 Low	FW: Question about moving into a new role and readjust...	Jun 26	no date	None		
☐ 0 Low	Study new tax laws	Jun 22	no date	None		
☐ 0 Low	sign up for advanced MYN training	Jun 22	no date	None		

MYN settings *manually*, and I spend almost 20 pages in my Outlook books showing users how. So, be thankful that ToodleDo does all this for you with one quick setting!

Figure 7 shows how your ToodleDo list should look once you turn on the MYN configurations. Notice the Start Date field and the descending sorting of the start dates. That's exactly what you want to see—it's FRESH Prioritization in action.

Mobile Settings

By the way, if you are using the mobile apps for ToodleDo—the ones I introduced in Chapter 7—you may recall that in the videos for those apps I suggested that you, as an option, make the setting to hide tasks with future start dates. I did that in anticipation of this advanced chapter, so you wouldn't have to go back and configure that later.

Well, now you know exactly why I suggested you do that: if you did, your mobile solutions are already set and ready to go. However, if you skipped that option, now is the time to watch those videos again and tweak the software to make those changes.

Bigger Things: Managing Your Significant Outcomes on Your To-Do List

Now is a good time to raise a topic that will fine-tune the way you manage your tasks and workday.

As you learned early in this book, 1MTD is based on managing *urgency*. For example, you use urgency zones as the primary way to organize your tasks. The main purpose of 1MTD is to make sure that you get urgency under control so that you can focus on your more important work with a calmer state of mind and a more creative perspective.

So, once you get urgency under control, where do you list the larger, more important things that you need to get done during the week? In other words, when you've put out the fires, what next things do you focus on to get back to your main work? Where do you list the larger accomplishments you wish to make progress on this week and beyond?

I call these larger accomplishments Significant Outcomes, or SOCs for short. If you think about it, they don't really fit in the three urgency zones. For example, they don't belong in the Critical Now section because most of these are not critically due today. And if you list them in the Opportunity Now section they may get lost among the smaller to-dos that you have listed there. So, I recommend you list them *separately* from the three urgency zones.

If you are using the paper system that I showed you in Chapter 2, I recommend you create a section above the three urgency zones labeled Significant Outcomes, and list there the three or four large accomplishments you want to make progress on this week. In fact, my advanced Word

1MTD templates do this. If you are using the paper system, you can download them from the following link.

Go to: www.1MTD.biz/1MTD-TemplateAdv.doc

Showing SOCs in ToodleDo

But I assume you are using ToodleDo at this point and luckily ToodleDo has a very good way to show SOCs. How? Well, we use a new Priority field level in ToodleDo.

You may have noticed that ToodleDo has five priority levels assignable within its Priority field, and we've been using only three of them so far: High, Medium, and Low. One of the additional priority levels is called Top and we can use it in our system. So, what we're going to do is assign the priority Top to any item that we want to designate as a SOC for the week—just do that when you create the tasks. Then, in the browser version of ToodleDo, these items will sort above your urgency zone list and stand out prominently. Figure 8 shows how that looks in your task list.

Using SOCs

Using the Top priority to indicate Significant Outcomes, highlight items that represent relatively major efforts you have under way that you want to make progress on this week. These might be projects you are working on or large deliverables due later in the week.

Figure 8. ToodleDo with Significant Outcomes (SOCs) included

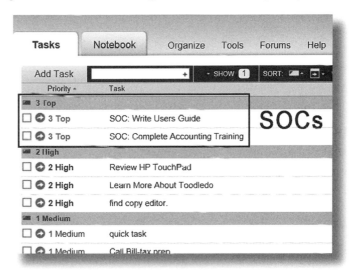

Once you start using SOCs, you'll get in the following habit: you'll get your urgent items under control, you'll take a deep breath, and then you'll look at your SOC list and start working on them. You'll also get in the habit of reserving the urgency zone items (the High, Medium, and Low priority items) for smaller next-action tasks; you'll put all other larger project-style tasks in the SOC list.

But don't get carried away. I recommend having no more than three or four SOCs in your list for the week; if you have more, they become a blur. To shorten your current list, you can set future start dates on some of your SOCs to hide them until a later date when you may have time to work on them.

Going Mobile with SOCs

The separate Top priority section that I showed in Figure 8 also shows up in the iPhone and iPad mobile versions of ToodleDo. So, you can use those mobile apps to highlight your SOCs while on the road.

However, the Android and BlackBerry third-party applications that I recommend (Pocket Informant) do *not* recognize the Top priority designation—that level does not exist in the Priority field list. If you create a Top priority item on your browser version of ToodleDo and then sync it with Pocket Informant, the mobile software treats that item as though it were set at High in the Priority field, and merges it with all the other tasks in the High priority section. Then they do not stand out as they should.

There is a way to work around that: when you enter your SOCs in ToodleDo, just type "SOC:" at the beginning of the subject line, followed by the task name. For example, "SOC: Finish Quarterly Report." That way these items stand out inside the High priority section that you view inside Pocket Informant.

More about Deadlines

Recall that I said you should not set a due date on every task? I commented that most tasks in fact do not have deadlines. But some do, so you may be wondering when and how to show deadlines on tasks. Let's talk about that.

Put Deadlines on Significant Outcomes

First, some background. The reason most tasks do not have true deadlines is that the true deadlines usually reside in the larger outcomes that you're trying to reach. If a big project is coming due, the project itself has a deadline, but the smaller pieces leading up to that completion have more flexibility regarding when you can complete them. So, it makes sense to put deadlines on your SOC tasks (the Top priority in ToodleDo) but not on all the tasks that you list in your urgency zone tasks (the High, Medium, and Low priority tasks).

Use DUE Notation

That said, some of the tasks in your urgency zone list will in fact have deadlines. So, how do you show those?

One way is to do it as I suggested at the beginning of this book; you simply type the due date right in front of the subject line of the task. So, for example, "DUE April 15 Tax Submission." Then set the start date well ahead of the deadline so you see the task early. That way, as this task floats in your to-do list for a while, every time you review your list you'll see that deadline notation and you'll pay attention to it—especially as the actual deadline gets closer. On the morning the deadline arrives, if it's still not done, move the item to the Critical Now section.

Put Some Deadlines on Your Calendar

Some deadlines require additional work at the time the task is to be turned in. For example, a report may require printing and collating as the last stage of the work—that may take an hour or more. In cases like this, I recommend you put an entry on your calendar to set aside the time needed to do that final work on the deadline day. And you may want to set a reminder alert that pops up on or before the appointment to remind you to start work on it early.

ToodleDo's Due Date Field

ToodleDo also has a Due Date field built in to its system. This is another place where I like ToodleDo better than Outlook. In Outlook, the Due Date field is linked to the Start Date field in a way that makes the Due Date field unusable if you use a start date. That's because it forces you to set a due date on any task that has a start date set on it; once you set the Start Date field, Outlook automatically populates the Due Date field—you cannot leave it blank. Since all our tasks in the MYN system have a start date, that makes it look like they all have due dates even when they don't. For that reason, I tell my students to ignore the Due Date field when using Outlook tasks with MYN.

But in ToodleDo there is no link between the Start Date and Due Date fields—that means you can use the Due Date field *effectively* for setting deadlines. In fact,

ToodleDo has a number of built-in features that help you track due dates. Here are a few:

- If a task has a Due Date field set, ToodleDo will turn those fields red when that date arrives.
- ToodleDo has a number of optional *views* you can activate that will highlight tasks with upcoming due dates. Just click the Due Date label at the top-left of the ToodleDo window to find them.
- ToodleDo also has an optional reminder feature that prompts ToodleDo to send you an SMS message or an e-mail message at the date and time the task is due.

Describing how to use all these features is beyond the scope of this book. For detailed instructions, check out my "Full" ToodleDo class at the link I showed you earlier and that I repeat here: www.1MTD.biz/extras

Defer-to-Review

Recall that the Over-the-Horizon list is a great place to store excess tasks that you don't have time to work on this week. By using it, you can easily get your Opportunity Now list down to 20 or fewer items. Since you check the Over-the-Horizon list only once per week, its larger size is not such an issue.

But after a while, your Over-the-Horizon list will get so big that you won't want to review it even once per week; perhaps yours has gotten that big already. If so, it's time for you to start using a new MYN process called *Defer-to-Review.*

Background

Much of what we've talked about in this chapter has been ways to manage a long list of Opportunity Now items. Using the Start Date field creatively was our main way of doing that. For example, setting future start dates helps decrease the size of the Opportunity Now list. And sorting newer start dates to the top (FRESH Prioritization) makes sure the most important tasks are at the top of the Opportunity Now list.

That said, you still should keep the Opportunity Now list below about 20 items; if it contains more than that you will not review it completely each day. So, moving items to the Over-the-Horizon section is your main way of getting the Opportunity Now list below 20 items.

But that gets us back to the problem—the Over-the-Horizon section will, after a few months, get too big to review even once a week; you'll just give up. At that point you need to adopt a new process for the Over-the-Horizon tasks. That process is called Defer-to-Review and it works great in an automated system like ToodleDo.

How Defer-to-Review Works

The way it works is simple: you make one change in how you place items in the Over-the-Horizon list. As before, you set the priority to Low to move a task there. But the change is this: you set a start date on that item *to a future date when you next want to review it.* That's it. Now, since these start dates are future dates, given the settings we just made in this chapter, those tasks will be *hidden* until that date arrives. The result is you will only have a few tasks to review each week in the Over-the-Horizon section—problem solved!

What future start dates should you use? For some items, your desired next review date may be next week (if it's really important). But most items you don't need to review every week. Most items can wait several weeks; many can wait several months between reviews because they just aren't that important.

For example, perhaps you wanted to check in with a sales prospect, and it really should be done as soon as possible, but you moved it to the Over-the-Horizon section because this week was just too packed. That one you probably want to review again next week. In contrast, let's say you have a wish-list task like "redecorate the office." That one you may only want to review season-ally—say, every three months. Defer-to-Review is perfect for making these distinctions and so keeping your weekly review load low.

One other thing. Since your Over-the-Horizon reviews are normally done on Mondays, you should be sure to set the future review dates to some future Monday. That way all the items pop up only on that day of the week. Or, if your review date is a different day, use that day of the week instead.

One result of Defer-to-Review is that your Monday review will now be a bit different. Each Monday a small number of Over-the-Horizon tasks will pop into the Low priority section of ToodleDo. You should then process each task as follows: if the task can and should wait longer, set a new future start date on the task and it will disappear again. Or, if the task needs more urgent attention this week, set the priority to High or Medium and that will move it into the upper section of your 1MTD. Keep processing each task like that until your Over-the-Horizon section is completely emptied; then repeat this each week.

And that's it; that's how to get control of a long Over-the-Horizon list. With this new process you only see a few Over-the-Horizon tasks each week—only those that need attention. No longer will an overflowing task list haunt you!

For more detailed instructions on Defer-to-Review in ToodleDo, check out my "Full" ToodleDo video training at the link I showed you earlier.

Go to: www.1MTD.biz/extras

And Defer-to-Review works in Outlook as well; how to do that is covered in all the Outlook training options shown at the end of Chapter 5.

Wrap-up

This was the longest chapter in the book, but for good reason. It taught you all the things you need to get you to the next level of task management—the MYN level. You may want to study this chapter again, after you have used the system for a few weeks. That way you will get the most out of the material here.

10

Reviewing the
One Minute To-Do List

That's it! You've just learned the complete 1MTD system, and I bet you are feeling that your workday is now well under control. If you've done this correctly, you now have a nice compact list that shows you what you need to do next and how urgent those tasks are. Everything else is well scheduled and out of sight so it doesn't add unnecessary stress to your day.

You are confidently adding items to that list as you get them and then only working them in priority order. You're no longer working on tasks just because you see them in front of you. Rather, you know the true urgency of your tasks now—you are working the ones that truly need urgent attention and postponing the ones that do not. And with your urgent tasks either scheduled or completed, you are calmly focusing on your most important work, your significant outcomes—you are making great progress on those things that really matter at work.

You are also transferring action e-mails to your to-do list so that you can track them along with the other work you need to do—in priority order. As a result, you no longer waste time doing low-priority e-mail actions just because they are in front of you.

All these simple yet powerful processes work. They allow you to feel and *be* in control and well ahead of your work.

Review of 1MTD Rules

Let's quickly review how to use 1MTD; doing so will help solidify the principles.

Urgent tasks that must be completed today are put in the Critical Now section; that's the High priority section in ToodleDo and Outlook. Tasks that you would like to do today or this week but that can wait up to ten days are placed in the Opportunity Now section; that's the Medium priority section in ToodleDo and the Normal priority section in Outlook. And tasks that can wait ten days or longer, perhaps much longer, are placed in the Over-the-Horizon section; this is the Low priority section in ToodleDo and Outlook.

To keep the size of this list well controlled, you should have no more than five items in the Critical Now list, and likely much fewer. You should have no more than 20 items in the Opportunity Now list. And you'll place all other items in the Over-the-Horizon section.

You will review the Critical Now section approximately once per hour. You will review the Opportunity Now section at least once per day. And you will review the Over-the-Horizon section once per week. And to keep the size of the Over-the-Horizon section under control, you'll use the Defer-to-Review process for setting future start dates at reasonable review cycles for each task.

And you'll try to write all tasks as next actions—the very next distinct step you can take that will move a task forward.

Those are the key rules. As you can see, this is a very simple system. With a little effort, you can get a huge amount of control over your workday.

Because the system is so effective, I encourage you to immediately start using it as the *one* place you keep all your tasks. This means that as tasks arrive in your in-box you copy them into your task system and manage them along with your other tasks. This also means that if tasks arrive in your voicemail you make a notation for each in your to-do list. If you have tasks that you jotted down in meeting notes or from phone calls or even from hallway conversations, immediately place those tasks in your list so you can track them as well. A serene sense of control will surround you once you can clearly see everything you need to do in one succinct list. It is the essence of workday control. Start using this list for all your tasks today.

Next Steps

If you have used the 1MTD for a while and are ready to learn more, consider some of the advanced resources that we offer on our website. For example, there is a lot more to learn about ToodleDo; the "Full" ToodleDo training I mentioned earlier goes well beyond what is covered in this book (see that on the book's "extra's" page at: www.1MTD.biz/extras).

And if you would like to take Outlook beyond what I showed you in Chapter 5, you'll definitely want to try out our offerings for that—doing so is really your only next step. Offerings include the Outlook book, self-study video training, and joining live webinars or public classes. If you manage a group at your place of work, consider having an onsite training for your entire group. Here is the link I showed you earlier that lists all these options.

Go to: www.1MTD.biz/outlook-classes.html

You can also use the contact information on the author's website (www.michaellinenberger.com) to reach a live person to discuss specific questions you may have.

In Conclusion

Congratulations on completing a powerful course of study. You've done well, you've learned how to manage your tasks, and you now have your workday under control.

It's surprising, isn't it? You used to think that a to-do list was just a simple list of items. But over time you probably found that it didn't work very well even if you used it consistently. Now you know that creating a to-do list requires a bit of intelligent thought—that there is a way to make it work. By using the new 1MTD principles, you really can keep your day under control; you really can get ahead of your day. Don't forget these simple principles—they may seem very basic but they are very, very powerful.

And even though it takes only one minute to review or add current tasks to your 1MTD list, sometimes you'll get behind in using it. If you do, don't despair. One of the nice things about this system is that if you get behind for a few days or even weeks, it's very easy to get caught up. All you need to do is review the core principles, sort the tasks into the three urgency zones, use the basic rules on how many tasks are allowed in each section, and you're there. You can usually dig out of the mess within a short amount of time. But it's better not to let yourself get behind in the first place—use this list every day and you'll be amazed at the sense of freedom it brings you. Enjoy the newfound confidence you gain in your ability to get things done. Recognize these life-changing skills you now have and use them regularly. You'll be glad you did!